# Promoting a safe church

# Promoting a safe church

Policy for safeguarding adults in the Church of England

CHURCH HOUSE PUBLISHING

Church House Publishing
Church House
Great Smith Street
London
SW1P 3AZ

ISBN-13 978 0 7151 4211 0

GS Misc 837

Printed in England by
Halstan & Co Ltd,
Amersham, Bucks

Published 2006 by Church House Publishing
Second impression 2009
Copyright © *The Archbishops' Council* 2006

Permission is granted for photocopies of the Confidential Declaration form (pp. 26–27) to be made by the purchaser. The remainder of this publication may not be reproduced or stored or transmitted by any means or in any form, electronic or mechanical, including photocopying, recording, or any information storage and retrieval system without written permission which should be sought from the Copyright Administrator, Church House Publishing, Church House, Great Smith Street, London SW1P 3AZ

Email: copyright@c-of-e.org.uk

# Contents

# Foreword
## by the Archbishops of Canterbury and York

Adults can need safeguarding too!

Quite properly we have put in a lot of effort over the past few years developing policies and procedures for the safeguarding of children and, while constant improvement is always necessary, we can be modestly proud of what has been achieved.

The time has now come to ensure that the Church can be as safe a place for adults as for children. That will only seem an odd comment if we forget that people are all vulnerable in one way or another and that an institution like the Church has special opportunities and challenges. Within the Church are 'all sorts and conditions' of human beings, diverse in age, gender, ethnicity and with different kinds of ability; there are professionals, amateurs and volunteers, there are ordained ministers and faithful members of congregations. The Church is a body whose members acknowledge their individual needs and which also recognises the human capacity for even the best to go wrong. Issues of power and dependence may not be greater in the Church than elsewhere, but we do have a unique responsibility and ability to address them.

We commend this document to the careful study of the Church as we seek to embody the very highest standards of care. Nothing less will do in a community called to witness to the eternal dignity of every human being.

✠ Rowan Cantuar:
✠ Sentamu Ebor:

# Summary of the Policy

- We are committed to respectful pastoral ministry to all adults within our church community.
- We are committed, within our church community, to the safeguarding and protection of vulnerable people.
- We will carefully select and train all those with any pastoral responsibility within the Church, including the use of Criminal Records Bureau disclosures where legal or appropriate.
- We will respond without delay to any complaint made that an adult for whom we were responsible has been harmed, cooperating with police and the local authority in any investigation.
- We will seek to offer informed pastoral care to anyone who has suffered abuse, developing with them an appropriate healing ministry.
- We will challenge any abuse of power by anyone in a position of trust.
- We will care for and supervise any member of our church community known to have offended against a vulnerable person.

# 1 Introduction

*Promoting a safe church* seeks to raise the awareness of members of the Church of England of the needs of adults both within society in general and more particularly within the church community. The document should be read in conjunction with the Church of England documents *Protecting all God's children* (2004) and *Responding to domestic abuse – guidance for those with pastoral responsibilities* (2006). Society is recognizing that people are being harmed when they are vulnerable for various reasons whether permanently or on a temporary basis and this abuse can take place in their own homes, in residential care, at work or in other activities including those provided by the Church. Some adults, who do not see themselves as 'vulnerable' under our working definition, may still find themselves exploited, bullied or abused. The safeguarding of adults when harm occurs is the responsibility of everyone. Awareness of the ways people can suffer harm encourages church members to be vigilant both within and outside the church community.

There is a particular responsibility for members of the Church to ensure that all people are treated with respect and that any complaints against church workers are dealt with promptly and fairly. Safeguarding adults within the Church is based on sound pastoral care and good practice.

This policy document is addressed to everyone in the Church of England but especially to church workers who have some responsibility for the pastoral care of others. Such workers may be ordained or lay, licensed, commissioned or accredited; they may be volunteers with no official authorization. This document is intended to help members of the Church to consider issues of vulnerability, disability and integration. Understanding the needs of people with vulnerabilities will enhance pastoral ministry, whilst information about what constitutes mistreatment of adults will be a necessary part of ministerial training. Certain groups, for example ordained clergy and employed people, might already have structures within which they work. The codes and procedures outlined in this document are therefore particularly relevant to those who work or volunteer in more informal ways. Harassment by work colleagues is also covered. For the purposes of this document the term 'church worker' is used to cover all categories.

## 1.1 Context

In recent years society as a whole has become more aware of the extent of harm to adults. In response to this Parliament passed the Care Standards Act 2000[1] and the Department of Health published accompanying guidance *No Secrets*, a document developing and implementing inter-agency policies and procedures to protect vulnerable adults. The guidance provides a framework for the safeguarding of adults, including recommended structures for the investigation of allegations of abuse by local authorities. Voluntary organizations such as churches are also asked to develop similar procedures if they are providing services or are in regular contact with adults who might be vulnerable. More recent government guidance, *Safeguarding Adults: a national framework of standards and good practice in adult protection work*, published in October 2005, expands the guidance in *No Secrets*.

In 2002 Churches Together in Britain and Ireland produced the report *Time for Action*, which in part challenged the Churches to respond more compassionately and effectively to adults who had been sexually abused in a church context. This present paper is a response to all three documents *No Secrets*, *Safeguarding Adults* and *Time for Action*.

## 1.2 Vulnerability

Human beings are, by their very nature, subject to the chances and changes of this world. Each one has strengths and weaknesses, capacities and restrictions. At some time everyone will be vulnerable to a wide range of pressures, concerns or dangers. No one is 'invulnerable'; some people may consider themselves to be strong but, when circumstances change, strengths can quickly disappear. Some people by reason of their physical or social circumstances have higher levels of vulnerability than others. It is the Christian duty of everyone to recognize and support those who are identified as being more vulnerable. In supporting a vulnerable person we must do so with compassion and in a way that maintains dignity. Vulnerability is not an absolute; an individual cannot be labelled as 'vulnerable' in the same way as a child is regarded as such. Childhood is absolute: someone who is not yet eighteen years of age is, in the eyes of the law,[2] a child; this is not the case with vulnerability. Some of the factors that increase vulnerability include:

- a sensory or physical disability or impairment;
- a learning disability;
- a physical illness;
- mental ill health (including dementia), chronic or acute;
- an addiction to alcohol or drugs;
- the failing faculties in old age;
- a permanent or temporary reduction in physical, mental or emotional capacity brought about by life events, for example bereavement or previous abuse or trauma.

## 1.3 Definitions for use with those who may be vulnerable

In order to bring into focus those people for whom the Church should have a particular care this working definition may be helpful:

**Any adult aged 18 or over who, by reason of mental or other disability, age, illness or other situation is permanently or for the time being unable to take care of him or herself, or to protect him or herself against significant harm[3] or exploitation.**

A narrower definition is in use for the particular purpose of applying to the Criminal Records Bureau,[4] but it should be noted that the latest government guidance *Safeguarding Adults* does not speak of 'vulnerable adults', which puts the onus on the victim of abuse, but rather concentrates on enabling adults to 'retain independence, well being and choice and to access their human right to live a life that is free from abuse and neglect'.[5]

## 1.3 A definition of mistreatment, abuse and harm[6]

**Mistreatment** is defined in *No Secrets* as 'a violation of an individual's human and civil rights by any other person or persons'. In a church context it could be any misuse of a pastoral or managerial relationship, from the most serious to less severe behaviour, which lies at its root. The term covers **abuse**, bullying and harassment. These categories are not watertight and can merge into one another. **Harm** is what results from mistreatment or abuse.

## 1.4 Our theological approach[7]

From beginning (in the cry of a baby) to end (in the cry from the cross), the life and death of Jesus Christ illustrates the willingness of God to be vulnerable in order to share to the full our world of pain, poverty, suffering and death. In his earthly ministry, Jesus constantly showed himself to be compassionately on the side of the outcast, the marginalized and the stranger, reaching across social barriers with the inclusive love of God. This was wholly in line with the Hebrew Bible's priority concern for orphans and widows, its obligation to provide a voice for the voiceless, and its prophetic call for justice to 'roll down like waters, and righteousness like an ever-flowing stream' (Amos 5.24). The risen Christ's commission to his followers ('As the Father has sent me, so I send you' [John 20.21]) requires the Christian Church to exercise that same concern for those whom some in society treat as the outsider and the stranger, to reach across barriers of exclusion and demonstrate a love which shows itself in compassionate pastoral care and in the quest for justice in all our relationships. The heart of Christian pastoral care is this: love for God and love for our neighbour, the social expression of which is justice in all human affairs.

In line with the gospel of creation and redemption, Christian pastoral care has often been described in terms of healing, sustaining and reconciling. All people, and especially those who may be marginalized through a vulnerability, need to receive the healing love of God to rebuild relationships with others or within themselves which illness, disability or abuse may have fractured. Healing is a process of being made more whole. There can be substantial steps for some people in this life, which can be aided through the Church's ministry of healing and reconciliation, though full healing in all dimensions of life must wait for the coming of Christ's kingdom when all creation will be healed and renewed. For those who have been abused, neighbour love includes the need for them to be listened to and believed, supported as they cope with the effects of trauma, enabled to make the choices which will lead to healing and start on the costly road towards forgiveness. The Christian gospel offers the grace of reconciliation with God, which can enable people to learn to live lives more reconciled with others and with their environment.

Everyone needs the sustaining reassurance that they are treated with the respect that is due to all human beings made in the image of God and precious to God. Those who have challenging personal situations must receive the resources they need to live independent lives with dignity. Everyone needs to know that they can live safely in a non-threatening environment.

Christian pastoral care takes place in the context of the present world, which in gospel terms is provisional. We live in the time between God's living Word to us in Jesus Christ, and the coming of God's kingdom in its fullness, when there will be no more pain, no more tears, no more social exclusion, and no more death. In this world the Holy Spirit sustains our ministry – enabling us to do what we can within the constraints of fallenness and sin, and yet holding out the living hope that the day will come when God will be all and in all.

# 2 The Policy

## 2.1 Principles underlying the Policy

Christian communities should be places where all people feel welcomed, respected and safe from abuse. The Church is particularly called by God to support those at the margins, those less powerful and those without a voice in our society. The Church can work towards creating a safe and non-discriminatory environment by being aware of some of the particular situations that create vulnerability. Issues which need to be considered include both the physical environment and the attitudes of workers. A person who might be considered vulnerable has the right to:[8]

- be treated with respect and dignity;
- have their privacy respected;
- be able to lead as independent a life as possible;
- be able to choose how to lead their life;
- have the protection of the law;
- have their rights upheld regardless of their ethnicity, gender, sexuality, impairment or disability, age, religion or cultural background;
- be able to use their chosen language or method of communication;
- be heard.

## 2.2 The House of Bishops Policy Statement on safeguarding adults in the Church of England

The Church of England is committed to encouraging an environment where all people and especially those who may be vulnerable for any reason are able to worship and pursue their faith journey with encouragement and in safety. Everyone, whether they see themselves as vulnerable or not, will receive respectful pastoral ministry recognizing any power imbalance within such a relationship.

All church workers involved in any pastoral ministry will be recruited with care including the use of the Criminal Records Bureau disclosure service when legal or appropriate. Workers will receive training and continuing support.

Any allegations of mistreatment, abuse, harassment or bullying will be responded to without delay. Whether or not the matter involves the church there will be cooperation with the police and local authority in any investigation.

Sensitive and informed pastoral care will be offered to anyone who has suffered abuse, including support to make a complaint if so desired: help to find appropriate specialist care either from the church or secular agencies will be offered.

Congregations will often include people who have offended in a way that means they are a continuing risk to vulnerable people. The risks will be managed sensitively with the protection of adults and children in mind.

## 2.3 Implementing this Policy – a checklist

The government guidance *No Secrets* provides the following checklist showing the responsibilities of those who have contact with or provide services for vulnerable people. It provides an action plan for the Church. We should:

- Seek to work in a non-abusive way that respects the rights of individuals to enjoy privacy, dignity, independence and choice. See Good practice recommendations.
- Actively promote the empowerment and well-being of vulnerable people through the services we provide. See Good practice recommendations.
- Ensure rigorous recruitment practices to deter those who actively seek vulnerable people to exploit or abuse, including taking up references and using CRB checks. See Procedure 1.
- Actively promote an organizational culture within which all those who express concern will be treated seriously and will receive a positive response from management. See Procedure 2.
- Ensure that staff and volunteers understand that vulnerable people can be abused and that they know what to do if they think that someone is being abused. See Procedure 2 and Appendix 2.
- Ensure that all staff and volunteers receive appropriate training and support.
- Have an internal policy, procedure and guidance on how managers, staff and volunteers will deal with allegations of abuse, including allegations against their own organization's staff and volunteers. Ensure that the procedure links to the local inter-agency procedure. See Procedure 2.
- Work in cooperation with the local Adult Services[9] and the police when they are investigating an allegation of abuse. See Procedure 2.
- Identify a 'lead officer' who takes responsibility for training staff and volunteers and updating procedures. See Section 2.4 Implementing a policy in a diocese and Section 2.5 Implementing a policy in a parish.
- Ensure that confidentiality and information sharing related to the protection of vulnerable adults and perpetrators of abuse in a multi-agency context are maintained through the agreed protocols. See Appendix 1.

**Have other policies and procedures in place which support good practice, e.g. complaints / whistle blowing / management of service users' money / staff disciplinary procedures. See Procedure 3 and Good practice recommendations, especially GP2.6.**

Those organizations that provide a service commissioned by the local authority may well find that their responsibility to report abuse using the local inter-agency procedures will be a contractual requirement.

Those organizations that are the subject of regulatory authorities (e.g. the Commission for Social Care Inspection) will also have additional statutory responsibilities with respect to their duty to report abuse and recruitment of staff.

**NB** All organizations also have a responsibility to report any concerns that staff and volunteers may have about the abuse of a child or young person (under 18) to the local authority Children's Service. See *Protecting all God's children* (2004).

## 2.4 Implementing a policy in a diocese

It is recommended that each diocese appoint someone to act in respect of adults. The duties of such a person would include helping people to understand the nature of vulnerability, being the person to whom people in parishes can bring their concerns, and promoting the training of those working in this area. It is likely that there is already in post someone who has the interests of adults with particular vulnerabilities as part of their remit. They could liaise with the child protection adviser, especially in regard to referrals and recruitment decisions. In some dioceses it may be appropriate, possible and cost-effective for the child protection adviser to take on a role in the safeguarding of adults. Such a lead person in the diocese should discuss this policy with the member of staff with responsibility for safeguarding adults in the adult services department of the local authority (county, borough or unitary) in order that they understand local procedures and are clear about the best route for reporting concerns. The implementation of this policy will need to be monitored by the diocese from time to time.

## 2.5 Implementing a policy in a parish

Everyone, as a citizen, has a responsibility for the safety, well-being and protection of others. Everyone within the church community also has a responsibility to ensure that there is a welcome for all people, including those seen as vulnerable. A policy about the safeguarding of vulnerable people should be the concern of the whole congregation and therefore should be presented to the Parochial Church Council for adoption and be reaffirmed at least annually. This is an opportunity for church members to remember their commitment to one another.

Everyone should be alert to situations where those who might be vulnerable are exposed to unacceptable risks. Those who work with vulnerable people often find themselves in challenging situations and need the support, prayers and encouragement of everyone in the congregation. Sometimes workers may be confronted with difficult behaviour on the part of those with whom they are working; sometimes workers may have to face difficult decisions about incidents that may need to be reported to the statutory authorities. The congregation and church workers need to be clear about the procedures which should be followed when there are concerns about people being harmed or abused.

Those who work most closely with vulnerable people in lunch clubs, day centres, Bible study groups or as pastoral visitors, etc., are in a unique position to get to know them. As a result workers might learn about things that give cause for concern or they may see others, sometimes including fellow workers or church members, behaving in ways that may be described as abusive or potentially harmful. When visiting a care home, for example, a visitor may observe another resident showing signs of abuse. Workers should have a good knowledge of the guidelines for good practice and should be implementing them; they should know what to do if they learn of any incidents where vulnerable people are being mistreated or abused.

Not all concerns about the welfare or safety of a vulnerable person need the public authorities to be involved;[10] sometimes it may be that the concern focuses on behaviour and attitudes that are not immediately harmful and then the matter should be dealt with through training or discussion. The choices of the adult concerned should if at all possible be accepted. The response to any concerns should always be proportionate and appropriate to the issue.

Parishes should do their best to provide a safe place for those who may be vulnerable. Where the parish organizes special activities or groups for vulnerable people, care should be taken to ensure that those who work in these activities are carefully appointed, supported and supervised. Recruitment to other positions of trust should be carried out sensitively but thoroughly to try to prevent inappropriate appointments being made.

The Parochial Church Council together with the incumbent carries a duty of care for the safety of those who attend or use the church. The Council should, with the help of the diocese, ensure that a policy is in place that reflects the need to safeguard vulnerable people and that it is being implemented and has appropriate resources. The Council needs to find ways to communicate the policy to the whole congregation. Clergy in particular need to be aware of the pastoral needs of vulnerable people, their carers and those that work with them.

It is recommended that a named individual be appointed by the PCC to act as the key person to speak on behalf of vulnerable people both within the congregation and to outside bodies. Ideally the appointed person should have some experience in this field. They should be recruited using Procedure 1 and they should apply for a CRB disclosure. Such a person may be the most appropriate person to receive information about concerns and will need to listen carefully, possibly discussing the matter with the adult concerned and making a decision about whether these concerns should be passed to an outside statutory body such as the police or the local authority Adult Services. The lead person should always liaise with and seek advice from the designated person in the diocese. If there is clear evidence that the vulnerable person has suffered abuse, then this should be reported as soon as possible to local authority Adult Services as the lead agency. All Adult Services Departments (or similar) have policies about the safeguarding of vulnerable peoples and will work in multi-agency collaboration with the health service and police.

Some parishes may find it difficult to appoint someone to undertake this responsibility. It may be more appropriate for this to be considered as an appointment within each deanery. However it must be remembered that each PCC is legally responsible for the activities in its own parish.

## 2.6 A model policy statement on the safeguarding of adults in a parish

**Policy on the Safeguarding of Adults in the Church**

This statement was adopted by ........................ (Parish) at a Parochial Church Council meeting held on ................

This policy will be reviewed each year to monitor the progress which has been achieved.

1. We recognize that everyone has different levels of vulnerability and that each of us may be regarded as vulnerable at some time in our lives.
2. As members of this parish we commit ourselves to respectful pastoral care for all adults to whom we minister.
3. We commit ourselves to the safeguarding of people who may be vulnerable, ensuring their well-being in the life of this church.
4. We commit ourselves to promoting safe practice by those in positions of trust.
5. The parish commits itself to promoting the inclusion and empowerment of people who may be vulnerable.
6. It is the responsibility of each of us to prevent the physical, emotional, sexual, financial and spiritual abuse of vulnerable people and to report any such abuse that we discover or suspect.
7. We undertake to exercise proper care in the appointment and selection of those who will work with people who may be vulnerable.
8. The parish is committed to supporting, resourcing, training and regularly reviewing those who undertake work amongst people who may be vulnerable.
9. The parish adopts the guidelines of the Church of England and the Diocese.
10. Each person who works with vulnerable people will agree to abide by these recommendations and the guidelines established by this church.

This church appoints ........................... to represent the concerns and views of vulnerable people at our meetings and to outside bodies.

Incumbent ........................................................................

Churchwarden ..................................................................

Churchwarden ..................................................................

Date ..............................................................................

*Good practice recommendations 1*

# Promoting good practices working with people who may be vulnerable

Promoting a safe church is not so much a matter of procedures and rules but rather working together, both helpers and those with differing vulnerabilities, to provide the right environment for everyone to grow in Christian faith. It is important that those working together agree on standards of conduct and how activities are to be carried out. This is particularly necessary if those adults involved in the activity cannot speak for themselves. Attitudes of respect and consideration should be developed in all work with adults, ensuring that everyone is able to maximize their life choices and independence. Privacy and confidentiality are important to everyone and especially people who are dependent on others for aspects of their everyday living.

Some other points to consider are:

- Helping in such a way as to maximize a person's independence. People with additional needs can and do lead active and fulfilled lives but some may need support and resources to do so.
- Always respecting the person and all their abilities.
- Recognizing the choices people make even if they may appear risky.
- Giving people the highest level of privacy and confidentiality possible in the circumstances.
- Including everyone in decisions affecting their life.
- Creating an environment within the Church that can include everyone.

Most people will have no difficulty accepting these values of independence, choice, inclusivity, privacy and respect. However, it is sometimes difficult to think how they might be put into practice. See Appendix 3 for further examples of good practice.

## GP1.1 Premises

Church buildings will be inspected to meet Health and Safety standards and should allow people with disabilities to participate as much as possible. Parishes should undertake a regular audit of their buildings in order to ensure that premises enable the church to carry out its duties under the Disability Discrimination Acts of 1995 and 2005. Issues of access, visibility, audibility and toilet facilities are among the items that should be addressed.

## GP1.2 Duty of care – insurance advice

All church workers have a duty of care towards those to whom they minister. National and diocesan good practice guidelines and the procedures in this document should be followed to ensure that insurance cover is maintained. The insurers should be contacted as soon as it is clear that a claim may be made against a diocese or parish.

## GP1.3 Prevention of abuse in the Church

Prevention is best achieved by both the careful training of workers and the provision of supervision or mentoring for all those working with vulnerable people. Church workers need to understand that they hold a position of power and influence even if they do not feel that that is the case.

Prevention can be particularly difficult with those who may be vulnerable, because of the range of people who are in contact with them and the variety of ways in which churches and others try to be of help or befriend people who otherwise would be isolated. The desire to provide a safe environment should not get in the way of allowing people to develop their own friendships and contacts – some of which may be felt to be risky. If people are working together in groups this can be one way in which harmful behaviours can be prevented. This is not, however. always the case and there have been many instances of a culture of abusive behaviour or attitudes developing in organizations or amongst groups of workers. Risks are increased when people have individual contact with those who are vulnerable.

## GP1.4 Worship

There are times when it is appropriate to hold services which have a focus on people with learning or other disabilities. In such instances the liturgy should not be demeaning or patronizing but should have the same aims as any other form of worship – those of reminding us of the presence of God, of saying sorry for our sinfulness, of adoring his majesty, and of coming closer to his presence.

The words that are used in such services may be different from the mainstream but the intent must not differ. It is vital, if planning such an event, to speak with the people who will attend, their families, friends and carers to ensure that everything is appropriate to the situation.

If a service is primarily aimed at deaf people, it is important to set the liturgy in a form that reflects the structure of British Sign Language. The pace of the worship should be sensitive to the requirements of the interpreters and, of course, deaf people should be fully involved in the planning and delivery of the service.

Regular worship in church should take account of the wide range of requirements of any congregation. As well as the church building offering full accessibility for people with mobility challenges, it is also important to cater for the requirements of other disabled people. Some examples might be that:

- **A proportion of all printed material should be in a sans-serif typeface no smaller than 12-point with the ink colour having a**

**very good contrast with that of the paper. About 10 per cent of all printed items should be in large print: 18-point sans-serif type in black on lemon-yellow paper. It is not acceptable to simply enlarge an existing document to twice the size and regard this as 'large print'.**

- **If possible printed material should also be available by electronic means in advance of the service to allow a person with impaired vision to read the document on a computer and then save it in whichever form is most convenient.**

- **All projected images should be audio-described and anyone presenting material on a screen should keep their faces towards the audience to enable lip-reading. Similarly, speakers should not cover their lips.**

*Good practice recommendations 2*

# Guidance for those in positions of trust or exercising pastoral ministry with vulnerable people

Many dioceses have produced helpful guidance on the professional conduct of clergy and lay people. The Convocations of York and Canterbury have also produced *Guidelines for the Professional Conduct of the Clergy*.

All those involved in pastoral ministry, whether paid or unpaid, clergy or lay, should be working within this or a similar set of guidelines. Following such guidelines should not only protect vulnerable people but also ensure that workers are not wrongly accused of abuse or misconduct.

## GP2.1 Pastoral relationships

Exercising any kind of ministry involves workers developing an understanding of themselves and how they relate to others, how they increase the well-being of others and how they ensure their own well-being and safety. People in positions of trust necessarily have power, although this may not be apparent to them, therefore respecting professional boundaries is particularly important. Many pastoral relationships can become intertwined with friendships and social contacts, making this guidance even more necessary.

- Church workers should exercise particular care when ministering to persons with whom they have a close personal friendship or family relationship.
- Church workers should be aware of the dangers of dependency in pastoral and professional relationships and seek advice or supervision when these concerns arise.
- Church workers who exercise a healing ministry should be trained in the theology and non-intrusive practice of that work.[11]
- Church workers should recognize their limits and not undertake any ministry that is beyond their competence or role (e.g. therapeutic counselling, deliverance ministry, counselling victims of abuse and domestic violence, or their perpetrators, or giving legal advice). In such instances the person should be referred to another person or agency with appropriate expertise.
- Church workers should avoid behaviour that could give the impression of inappropriate favouritism or the encouragement of inappropriate special relationships.

- Church workers should treat those with whom they minister or visit with respect, encouraging self-determination, independence and choice.
- Care should be taken when helping with physical needs, washing and toileting, always respecting the choices of the individual concerned.
- Pastoral relationships may develop into romantic attachments and such situations should be handled sensitively. Workers need to recognize such a development and make it clear to both the person concerned and a supervisor or colleague. Alternative arrangements should be made for the ongoing pastoral care of the person concerned.
- Church workers should not undertake any pastoral ministry while they are under the influence of drink or non-prescribed drugs.

## GP2.2 Conversations and interviews in a ministry context

Formal interviews and informal conversations in a ministry context are pastoral encounters. Church workers should be aware of their language and behaviour. For example, innuendoes or compliments of a sexual nature are always inappropriate. When a person asks questions or seeks advice around topics of a sexual nature, the worker should be discerning about the motives and needs of the person and question their own ability to assist.

The church worker should consider in advance:

- the place of the meeting, arrangement of the furniture and lighting, the worker's dress;
- the balance of privacy for conversation with the opportunity for supervision (open doors or windows in doors, another person nearby);
- the physical distance between people determined by hospitality and respect, being aware that someone may have suffered abuse or harassment in the past;
- whether the circumstances suggest a professional or social interaction;
- the propriety or danger of visiting or being visited alone, especially in the evening;
- the personal safety and comfort of all participants;
- establishing at the outset the nature of the interview in respect to subject matter, confidentiality and duration;
- the appropriateness of initiating or receiving any physical contact, for example gestures of comfort, which may be unwanted or misinterpreted.

## GP2.3 Record keeping and privacy

- Church workers should consider keeping a daily record of pastoral encounters to include date, time, place, subject and actions to be taken. The content of any encounter should only be recorded with the person's consent unless it is a matter of child protection or might be a record of suspicion of abuse or mistreatment.

- Any record should be factual and avoid rumour or opinion.
- Records concerned with abuse should be kept indefinitely (at least 50 years).
- The publishing, sharing or keeping of personal data or images should follow the appropriate legislation. See Appendix 1.

## GP2.4 Working with colleagues

The standards maintained within a pastoral relationship are equally relevant in relationships with colleagues. Harassment or bullying should never be condoned. All workers need to be aware of the possibility of stress within the work place. The needs of family should be acknowledged and all who work together should acknowledge the boundaries between work and home, allowing sufficient time for relaxation and holidays. Everyone who works with vulnerable people should know to whom they are accountable and have a designated person with whom to discuss their work.

- Church workers should be aware of the responsibilities, function and style of other church workers and encourage cooperation and consultation between workers in the tasks they do.
- Colleagues should not be discriminated against, harassed, bullied or abused for any reason.
- Colleagues should not be penalized for following this guidance or for taking action regarding others and this guidance.
- When leaving office or relinquishing any task church workers should relinquish any pastoral relationship except with the agreement of any successor.
- Church workers should know to whom they are accountable and be regularly mentored by them or another person who can assist. Such mentoring is especially necessary for those undertaking a continuing individual pastoral ministry of counselling, or when their ministry takes them outside normal church work.
- Church workers should ensure that their tasks can be carried out by another if they are ill or otherwise unable to fulfil their responsibilities.

## GP2.5 Sexual conduct

The sexual conduct of church workers may have an impact on their ministry within the Church. It is never appropriate for workers to take advantage of their role and engage in sexual activity with anyone with whom they have a pastoral relationship. Workers should be aware of the power imbalance inherent in pastoral relationships.

- Church workers must not sexually abuse an adult or a child.
- Church workers must take responsibility for their words and actions if wishing to make physical contact with another adult (e.g. a hug may be

misunderstood) or talk to them about sexual matters. This will include seeking permission, respecting the person's wishes, noticing and responding to non-verbal communication, refraining from such conduct if in doubt about the person's wishes.

- Church workers should follow the Church's discipline on sexual matters.
- Church workers must not view, possess or distribute sexual images of children and should refrain from viewing, possessing or distributing sexually exploitative images of adults.
- Church workers should avoid situations where they feel vulnerable to temptation or where their conduct may be misinterpreted.

## GP2.6 Financial integrity

Financial dealings can have an impact on the church and the community and must always be handled with integrity. Those with authority for such matters should maintain proper systems and not delegate that responsibility to anyone else.

- Church workers should not seek personal financial gain from their position beyond their salary or recognized allowances.
- Church workers should not be influenced by offers of money.
- Church workers should ensure that church and personal finances are kept apart and should avoid any conflict of interest.
- Money received by the church should be handled by two unrelated lay people.
- Any gifts received should be disclosed to a supervisor or colleague where it should be decided whether they could be accepted.
- Care should be taken not to canvass for church donations from those who may be vulnerable, e.g. the recently bereaved.

## GP2.7 Behaviour outside work and Christian ministry

In church ministry behaviour outside work can often impinge on that ministry. Church workers are expected to uphold Christian values throughout their lives.

*Good practice recommendations 3*

# Responding to disclosures by those who have experienced misuse of power, abuse or harassment

After experiencing abuse, at some time during the healing process many people will want to consider further action beyond personal acceptance of what has happened.

Such action may involve deciding to tell a trusted friend, partner, parent or perhaps a member of the clergy. However, some people have been further hurt when the friend, relative or church worker has not been able to cope with the disclosure and has responded inappropriately.

Seeking some kind of therapeutic help may be an option and it may be that within such help or discussions with friends consideration is given to what else needs to be done.

Abuse, which thrives on secrecy, loses some of its power to harm when this secrecy is broken. Nevertheless, whom to tell, when, and for what purpose needs careful thought. Being able to talk to a close friend or relative, who is able to hear, support and care, is for many people the most useful help in healing. For some this trusted relationship is with a counsellor, clergyperson or other professional.

At some point in the personal healing journey many survivors consider what they should do about the abuser. Some may wish to confront the abuser either personally or by letter, for others this is impossible, but they still may wish to ensure that the abuser is not in a position to harm others.

One of the consequences of speaking to others about the abuse is that they may have a responsibility to act. A family member may need to be sure that others in the family are safe. A friend may be aware that the abuser is involved with children or vulnerable people and be concerned for them. Organizations that work with children or vulnerable people will have policies with procedures that need to be followed if someone in the organization becomes aware of allegations of abuse.

For some it will be important that the person is brought to account for their actions through the criminal justice system, and if a criminal act has been committed this may be a necessary action that the church must take in order to protect others. Following an investigation, the alleged abuser may be charged and taken to court. It takes a lot of courage to give evidence in court and to accept the decision of the jury. Nevertheless many people feel relieved whatever the outcome that they have done their best and spoken out in public.

If the alleged abuse has taken place within the church the survivor may wish to make this known to someone in authority and this should be facilitated even in cases where a formal complaint is not made. If a formal complaint is made written statements will be required. If the case comes to a tribunal evidence may need to be given in person. It is important that the survivor is supported throughout this process: deciding what to do, making the formal complaint and giving evidence if necessary.

*Good practice recommendations 4*

# Care of adult survivors of abuse in the Church[12]

Many adults in the Church may be suffering from the effects of abuse – abuse they suffered in childhood or as adults, abuse of different kinds. The Church has a responsibility to support those people who may feel very vulnerable and whose vulnerability may open them up to further abuse. Some abuse may seem trivial to an onlooker, but the severity of abuse needs to be seen in terms of how the victim responded to the abuse both at the time and later.

## GP4.1 Statistics

Although numbers vary, some reports show that about 1 in 4 girls, and 1 in 9 boys are abused in childhood.[13] Key research in 21 countries found varying rates from 7 to 36 per cent of women and 3 to 29 per cent of men reporting they had been sexually abused as children.[14] One of the most rigorous UK studies found that 12 per cent of women and 8 per cent of men reported they had been sexually abused before the age of 16.[15] There is some evidence that there is considerable under-reporting from boys and men.

## GP4.2 Effects of abuse

Some survivors cope well with life and are able to live apparently 'normally'. Some, however, although they present a 'normal' face to the world, may well be suffering and sometimes be unable to say what their problem is – or even to know why they feel ill at ease and unable to feel a sense of peace and joy.

Some may show a range of symptoms such as:

- repeated bouts of depression;
- exhibiting anger and hostility – or being unable to connect at all with feelings;
- behaving like a victim – low self-esteem and putting themselves down and constantly apologizing;
- inability to get close to people, or wanting to be inappropriately close;
- disturbed sleep, nightmares and so on;
- tending to 'space out' (cutting off from reality);
- exhibiting fears, phobias and anxiety;
- self-harming (this is a way of coping, not something done 'to get attention');
- tending to feel an inappropriate amount of guilt and shame;

- sometimes relying on smoking, drugs, alcohol or medication;
- experiencing hallucinations and/or 'flashbacks' of the abuse;
- sometimes moving from one abusive relationship to another.

## GP4.3 Loss of trust

Adults and children who are abused can lose trust in those around them, especially if the abuse was within the home. (Most abuse is carried out by people known to the victim.) The loss of trust will profoundly affect the life of the survivor. They may decide (often unconsciously) never to trust anyone ever again – and this is likely to affect their faith and relationships.

## GP4.4 Why didn't you say so at the time?

Many survivors say nothing about the abuse for many years. Some have buried their memories so deeply within themselves that they have 'forgotten' what happened – especially if the abuse happened when they were very young.

Memories may be 'triggered' in a range of ways, for example:

- hearing about abuse on television;
- being in another abusive situation such as finding difficulties with a domineering employer;
- being in a situation where they feel powerless;
- feeling vulnerable, ill, under stress, or suffering from burnout;
- the death of their abuser or of one of their carers;
- the birth of their own child.

Few victims can report their abuse close to the event and so often reported abuse is about events of years ago, leading to difficulties with finding any proof of what happened. It is often one person's word against another, and the likelihood of the survivor getting justice is slim. However, some cases do go to court, but the experience can be devastating for both children and adults and they are likely to need considerable support.

## GP4.5 Pastoral care of survivors

An adult (or indeed a child) disclosing abuse is in a vulnerable state. **Above all they need someone to listen to them – and also to believe them. They may need to be 'heard' in different contexts and over several years.**

If there is a complex pastoral situation when an adult discloses abuse (e.g. a young person in their twenties accusing a church worker of sexually abusing them), it would be appropriate to find some support for the different parties involved, such as another survivor to support the person making the allegations.

There is no quick fix for healing from abuse and it is crucial that survivors:

- Are not pushed into forgiving too early. Forgiving their abuser/s is a complex process, and considerable damage can be done by treating forgiveness as something that they must do unreservedly and now.

- Are not put in a position of feeling even more guilty than they already do. Survivors tend to feel that the abuse was all their fault, particularly when there was more than one abuser.
- Are accepted as they are, however full of anger they may be. Anger can be seen as one step along the road to forgiveness – at least if they are angry they are starting to accept that the abuse seriously affected them and this can be a good starting point to move towards healing.
- Are given a sense that those within the church community who know about the abuse are 'with them' along the road to recovery. The journey can be very long and supporters are essential.

Survivors can benefit from professional counselling if that is available, but also joining a self-help group can provide the kind of long-term support needed. Survivors helping other survivors can be powerful and effective.

## GP4.6 Survivors and church

Many survivors have problems with attending church and it can be that some of those on the fringes of church communities include survivors.

There are some specific things that can be difficult:

- Saying the Lord's Prayer (believing that they must forgive immediately or God will reject them).
- Specific words can trigger unwanted feelings or images, such as 'Father', 'sin', 'let Jesus come into you', 'overshadow'.
- The Peace can frighten survivors because they often don't want to be touched, particularly hugged.
- The emphasis on sin can be so difficult that some survivors leave the Church altogether.
- Anointing and touch is very difficult for someone whose body boundaries have been violated.

Holy communion can be extremely problematic.

- Words such as 'blood' and 'body' can trigger memories of the abuse.
- Some can't cope with anyone behind them so queuing to get to the altar is difficult.
- Having to get physically close to others might lead to unwelcome smells, such as deodorant, aftershave or the smell of alcohol.
- It can be hurtful to kneel with a man standing over them delivering wine at crotch level.

Those who have been ritually or spiritually abused face particular difficulties. Triggers may include ritual symbols and equipment such as the altar, candles, chalice, crosses and crucifixes, the sacrificial lamb, etc. People abused by those in ministry may have been told it was ordained by God, a special service to those who serve the Lord, a blessing from God, Spirit-led, etc. Sensitivity, care and ideally informed input are needed to help people work through these issues to discover the liberating truth of the Gospel.[16]

The sense of pollution is frequently internalized. Some survivors even feel that if they go to church they will 'pollute' the service for others; such is their feeling of guilt and shame.

**It is important to recognize the vulnerability and possible 'childlike' state of survivors, especially when they are in crisis or the early stages of healing. They can be over-compliant and easily manipulated. Power abuse within pastoral care is a real danger here.**

## GP4.7 Inappropriate responses to survivors

There are examples of inappropriate responses to survivors in the report *Time for Action* (pp. 52 ff.) and these stories could be a basis for discussion about care of survivors with staff or PCC members.

It is inappropriate to

- tell a survivor it is her fault that she has lost her virginity;
- insist a survivor must forgive before he or she comes to communion;
- say to them, 'It was all so long ago, why don't you forgive and forget?';
- expect a survivor to move towards recovery without considerable support;
- tell a survivor that they cannot work with children or young people 'because abused people abuse others';
- have unrealistic expectations of healing such as 'We've prayed for you for over a year now so you must be better';
- try to arrange for the survivor to meet with the perpetrator or suggest reconciliation is a good thing – you could put someone in real danger;
- try to counsel survivors without having sufficient knowledge or awareness yourself of the dynamics and issues of abuse;
- use touch or anointing without clear boundaries and informed consent.

Survivors need time to work on their feelings and be able to accept that:

- it was not their fault;
- they haven't committed the unforgivable sin;
- they have no need to feel guilt and shame;
- God loves them unconditionally.

*Procedure 1*

# Recruitment of paid employees and volunteers

## P1.1 Introduction

This procedure concerns the safe recruitment of paid employees and volunteers in parishes who are to work with children or those who may be vulnerable (including vetting by the Criminal Records Bureau).

1. The PCC should agree on ways in which new employees and volunteers who are to work with children or vulnerable people will be recruited and appointed, and who will be involved in the process. Agreement should be reached on who will be responsible for taking up references, seeking a confidential declaration, and validating the identity of applicants for CRB disclosures; these tasks can be completed by different people.

2. Leaders of groups should inform the person managing recruitment of possible new employees or volunteers at an early stage so that these procedures can be followed.

3. In general people should be involved in the life of the parish for at least six months before being asked to help with work with children or vulnerable people.

4. People may visit groups on an occasional basis where it would be unrealistic to recruit them using this procedure. It is important that they are not made responsible for a group or left in sole charge.

5. Young people between the ages of 14 and 16 assisting as helpers should be treated as 'visitors' to a group; care should be taken to support and supervise these young people.

6. Young people between the ages of 16 and 18 assisting as helpers should be appointed in the same way as adults, but with their parents' permission.

## P1.2 Managing the process

1. For any position, draw up a job description, which will include a statement of the tasks and responsibilities and to whom the person will be accountable.

2. Decide whether or not any new appointment requires a disclosure from the CRB. For disclosures at the standard or enhanced level there must be an expectation that the role will include regular contact with children or with vulnerable adults complying with the CRB definition, see below.

3. Ask all applicants to fill in an application form, which should include information about the policies required by the CRB. These policies should be made available to the applicant on request. The form will enable

applicants to show their qualifications and experience for the tasks or position offered.

4. Seek two references including at least one that can comment on a person's suitability to work with either children or vulnerable people. If possible, ensure that one reference is from outside the present congregation. Obtain a reference from the incumbent of any previous church.

5. Interview the candidates. Interviews for volunteers are likely to be relatively informal but still need to ensure that the volunteer and the task are compatible and that the volunteer has the necessary skills to carry it out.

6. Ask each successful applicant to complete a confidential self-declaration form. This gives the individual the opportunity to declare any convictions or allegations at an early stage. It should be made clear to the applicant to whom the form should be returned and who will see any confidential information it contains. Information contained on a declaration should be discussed with the diocesan child protection adviser or the person designated by the diocese to deal with these matters for vulnerable people. The manager of the recruitment procedure should be informed when a satisfactory confidential declaration has been obtained.

7. Complete the CRB process if applicable to the post. The diocese will have detailed procedures for this procedure.

8. If applicants have lived outside the UK it is the responsibility of the parish to satisfy themselves through references or equivalent CRB procedures that they are suitable people to be appointed.

9. Once all the checks have been completed and the person is appointed, any contract, probationary period or commissioning should be agreed. The person appointed should be asked to adhere to any diocesan policy for the protection of either children or vulnerable people, including a code of conduct. Post holders should be offered training and support to carry out their tasks.

## P1.3 The Criminal Records Bureau definition of a vulnerable adult

The CRB defines a vulnerable adult as:

> A person aged eighteen or over who receives services of a type listed in paragraph 1) below and in consequence of a condition of a type listed in paragraph 2) below, has a disability of a type listed in 3) below:
>
> **The services are:**
>
> a) Accommodation and nursing or personal care in a care home
>
> b) Personal care or support to live independently in his or her own home
>
> c) Any services provided by an independent hospital, independent clinic, independent medical agency or National Health Service body
>
> d) Social care services, or

e) Any services provided in an establishment catering for a person with learning disabilities.

**The conditions are:**

- A learning or physical disability
- A physical or mental illness, chronic or otherwise including an addiction to alcohol or drugs, or
- A reduction in physical or mental capacity

**The disabilities are:**

- A dependency upon others in the performance of, or a requirement for assistance in the performance of basic physical functions,
- Severe impairment in the ability to communicate with others, or
- Impairment in a person's ability to protect him/herself from assault, abuse or neglect.

Those who regularly care for, train, supervise or are in sole charge of vulnerable people as described by the above definition are the only ones who should obtain a CRB Enhanced Disclosure.

**Many people who work with adults will not be able to be checked. The extra check with the Protection of Vulnerable Adults (POVA) list[17] is further restricted to those providing a service to vulnerable adults either in residential care, as a domiciliary agency or as an adult placement service.**

Therefore:

- People working in or regularly visiting care homes can apply for a disclosure plus POVA check through the care home if this is required by the home.
- People visiting vulnerable people (as defined by the CRB) in their homes can apply for a disclosure without a POVA check, that is, the counter-signatory should not tick either of the boxes adults or children in section Y of the application form.
- People working with adults but not with the most vulnerable should be carefully recruited and references taken up.

## P1.4 Confidential Declaration form

*To be completed by those wishing to work with children or vulnerable people.*

The Confidential Declaration form applies to beneficed clergy, those who hold the bishop's licence or permission to officiate, employees, ordinands and volunteers who are likely to be in regular contact with children or vulnerable people. This form is strictly confidential and, except under compulsion of law, will be seen only by those responsible for the appointment and, when appropriate, the diocesan/bishop's adviser for children and vulnerable people. All forms will be kept securely under the terms of the Data Protection Act 1998. If you answer yes to any question, please give details, on a separate sheet if necessary, giving the number of the question you are answering.

1. Have you ever been convicted of a criminal offence (including any spent convictions under the Rehabilitation of Offenders Act 1974)?

   YES ☐ NO ☐

   *Note: Declare all convictions, cautions, warnings or reprimands however old or whether you are at present under investigation by the police. Motoring offences that cannot be dealt with by a prison sentence need not be declared. Posts where the person is working or coming into regular contact with children or vulnerable adults are exempt from the 'Rehabilitation Act 1974'. Convictions obtained abroad must be declared as well as those from the UK.*

2. Have you ever been cautioned by the police, given a reprimand or warning or bound over to keep the peace?

   YES ☐ NO ☐

3. Are you at present under investigation by the police or an employer for any offence?

   YES ☐ NO ☐

4. Has your name been placed on the Protection of Children Act (POCA), List 99 or the Protection of Vulnerable Adults List (POVA), barring you from work with children or vulnerable people?

   YES ☐ NO ☐

5. Have you ever been found by a court exercising civil jurisdiction (including matrimonial or family jurisdiction) to have caused significant harm* to a child or vulnerable adult, or has any such court made an order against you on the basis of any finding or allegation that any child or vulnerable adult was at risk of significant harm from you?

   YES ☐ NO ☐

   *Note: Declare any finding of fact by a civil court that your actions have significantly harmed a child or vulnerable adult. Declare any court orders made on this basis.*

6. Has your conduct ever caused or been likely to cause significant harm to a child or vulnerable adult, or put a child or vulnerable adult at risk of significant harm?

   YES ☐ NO ☐

   *Note: Make any statement you wish regarding any incident you wish to declare.*

7. To your knowledge, has it ever been alleged that your conduct has resulted in any of those things?

   YES ☐ NO ☐

   If yes, please give details, including the date(s) and nature of the conduct, or alleged conduct, and whether you were dismissed, disciplined, moved to other work or resigned from any paid or voluntary work as a result.

   *Note: Declare any complaints or allegations made against you, however long ago, that you have significantly harmed a child, young person or vulnerable adult. Any allegation or complaint investigated by the police, Children's Services, an employer or voluntary body must be declared. Checks will be made with the relevant authorities.*

8. Has a child in your care or for whom you have or had parental responsibility ever been removed from your care, been placed on the Child Protection Register or been the subject of a care order, a supervision order, a child assessment order or an emergency protection order under the Children Act 1989, or a similar order under other legislation?

   YES ☐ NO ☐

   *Note: All these matters will be checked with the relevant authorities.*

9. Have you any health problem(s), which might affect your work with children or vulnerable adults?

   YES ☐ NO ☐

   *Note: Declare in confidence any health issues that may affect your ability to work with children or adults. This question is primarily intended to help you if you subsequently need to withdraw from work e.g. because of a recurring health issue.*

   * Significant harm involves serious ill-treatment of any kind including neglect, physical, emotional or sexual abuse, or impairment of physical or mental health development. It will also include matters such as a sexual relationship with a young person or adult for whom you had pastoral responsibility.

## Declaration

I declare that the above information (and that on the attached sheets **) is accurate and complete to the best of my knowledge.

Signed ..........................................................................................

Full name ......................................................................................

Date .......................................... Date of Birth ................................

Address .........................................................................................

..................................................................................................

** Please delete if not applicable. Please return completed form to: ...............

Before an appointment can be confirmed applicants may be required to provide an enhanced/standard disclosure from the Criminal Records Bureau – see incumbent or parish coordinator for details.

All information declared on this form will be carefully assessed to decide whether it is relevant to the post applied for and will only be used for the purpose of safeguarding children, young people or vulnerable adults.

*Procedure 2*

# Reporting mistreatment

Many clergy and lay people will visit vulnerable people. If they suspect that someone is being mistreated in some way, they should always take responsibility for doing something about their concerns. Some vulnerable people will find it difficult to disclose abuse and may need help to tell their story to someone they trust. An independent interpreter should be used if there is any kind of communication challenge. Careful listening is most important, without 'leading' someone with suggestions or 'closed' questions that may confuse the story. If someone discloses abuse it is important to receive the information without making a judgement or making a comment that may lead the individual to believe his or her word is doubted.

Talking to a member of the clergy, social responsibility adviser, senior member of a voluntary organization or the social or health care services may help to clarify the issues. A referral to the local authority may be necessary.

Under no circumstances should anything be done that might be construed as an investigation of the allegation, as action of this nature may contaminate evidence should a formal investigation by either the police or local authority be instigated.

Many vulnerable people rely on their carers for support, shelter and care and therefore the reporting of mistreatment needs to be undertaken with sensitivity.

**The government guidance *No Secrets* places on local authorities the responsibility to provide a structure for the investigation of harm to vulnerable people. It is therefore important that serious concerns are referred to the designated person in the Adult Services Department (or similar) of the local authority.**

## P2.1 What degree of abuse justifies referral to the local authority?[18]

When deciding whether a referral is necessary it is helpful to consider the concept of 'significant harm' introduced in the Children Act 1989, which provides the threshold for the state to intervene to investigate possible abuse. The Act states that

> harm should be taken to include not only ill treatment (including sexual abuse and forms of ill treatment which are not physical), but also the impairment of, or an avoidable deterioration in, physical, intellectual, emotional, social or behavioural development. In assessing the seriousness of abuse the following factors need to be considered:
>
> - the **vulnerability** of the individual;
> - the **nature and extent** of the abuse;
> - the **intent** of the alleged offender;
> - the **length of time** it has been occurring;

- the **impact** on the individual;
- the risk of **repeated or increasingly serious** acts involving this or other vulnerable adults.

## P2.2 Allegations against church workers

Church workers themselves may be suspected of mistreatment of an adult or another worker. Workers may not be following a code of conduct for church workers, an example of which is set on page 13. (If the alleged abuse or mistreatment is of a child under the age of 18 years the procedures set out in *Protecting all God's children* must be followed.) If the abuse of adult appears to be a criminal offence the police must be informed and a referral must be made to the local authority. Consideration should be given to whether the worker should be suspended during any investigation.

With less serious matters such as inappropriate behaviour or attitude not amounting to abuse, the worker's immediate superior should approach the worker and discuss the concern with them with the aim of identifying ways of improving the situation. The worker should be informed that disciplinary proceedings might be brought if there is no improvement. People suffering from mistreatment may wish to make a complaint. Dioceses should have procedures in place to allow complaints to be made. A possible complaints procedure is provided in Procedure 4.

### Record keeping

It is recognized that people may not make a complaint about abuse until many years after the event. It is therefore important in all circumstances where it has been considered that abuse might have taken place to make careful, factual records. It is recommended that records containing issues of child or adult abuse should be held for a minimum of 50 years. The people involved in such records should be informed that a record is being kept and if possible all parties should agree the record.

### Duty of care – insurance advice

All church legal bodies, usually the parish, have a duty of care towards those to whom they minister. National and diocesan good practice guidelines and the procedures in this document should be followed to ensure that insurance cover is maintained. The insurers should be contacted as soon as it is clear that a claim may be made against a diocese or parish.

## P2.3 Matters to consider following an investigation

An investigation into harm of an adult may result in a criminal conviction, disciplinary penalties, dismissal or resignation from a voluntary or paid position. Support of all concerned will need to be continued throughout the incident. Sometimes in less serious cases the person concerned will need appropriate training and extra supervision in order to be able to continue in their position.

Any abuse within the Church also creates second-order victims, those who experience a betrayal of the trust they have placed in those holding office of any kind. Members of congregations can, for example, feel let down and hurt when one of their leaders offends. Special care is required when a congregation is recovering from the effects of disclosure of abuse.

Great care will need to be taken if a person convicted of any relevant offence wishes to be employed or redeployed in a position working with the vulnerable, either adults or children. The diocesan procedures set up to deal with blemished CRB disclosures should be used to assess any relevance or risk.

*Procedure 3*

# Ministering to known offenders[19]

Recent research has shown that a disproportionately large number of convicted offenders against children and vulnerable people attend churches. The figures range from 25 per cent upwards. It is therefore possible for many congregations to have offenders amongst their worshippers, some of whom will be known. Not all will have committed sexual offences; some will have been guilty of neglect, physical or emotional abuse. The Church's duty to minister to all imposes a particular responsibility to such people. This must not however compromise the safety of children and those adults who may be vulnerable.

Where an offender is known, befriended and helped by a group of volunteers to lead a fulfilled life without direct contact with children or vulnerable adults the chances of re-offending are diminished and the Church has thus an important role in preventing abuse.

- When it is known that a member of the congregation has been accused or convicted of abusing children, young or vulnerable people the diocesan child protection adviser or the person designated to give advice on vulnerable people must be consulted, so that a safe course of action can be agreed. Because of the compulsive nature of sexual abuse it is expected that an agreement will be entered into with the offender.
- A frank discussion should be held with the offender, explaining that a small group from the congregation will need to know the facts in order to create a safe place for him or her. If possible the membership of the group should be agreed. Those needing to know are likely to include the clergy, churchwardens, Child Protection or vulnerable person's coordinator and any befriending volunteers. Anybody coordinating activities for vulnerable groups will need to be informed so that they do not inadvertently ask the person to volunteer.
- Consider whether, with the offender's agreement, the congregation should be told.
- It must be made clear that no one else should be informed of the facts without the offender's knowledge. The highest levels of confidentiality should be maintained.
- The group should offer support and friendship as well as supervision. They should endeavour to keep open channels of communication.
- It will be necessary to establish clear boundaries for both the protection of the young or vulnerable people and to lessen the possibility of the adult being wrongly accused of abuse. Prepare an agreement which includes:

- – attending designated meetings only;
- – sitting apart from children or vulnerable people;
- – staying away from areas of the building where vulnerable groups meet;
- – attending a house group where there are no children or vulnerable people;
- – declining hospitality where there are children or vulnerable people;
- – never being alone with children or vulnerable people;
- – never working with children or vulnerable people.

- Ask the offender to sign the agreement.
- Enforce the agreement – do not allow manipulation.
- Provide close support and pastoral care.
- Review the agreement at regular intervals.
- Ban the offender from church if the agreement is broken and tell other churches or the probation officer. If the person cannot be banned because they live in the parish, the advice of the diocesan registrar should be sought and a high level of supervision maintained.

In some cases offences only come to light after many years. In such situations great sensitivity will be required. It must, however, be remembered that there may still be a substantial risk to children or vulnerable people.

*Procedure 4*

# Handling complaints against church workers

The cost to someone of making a complaint may be very high. It is important, therefore, that the church takes complaints very seriously. Complaints should be dealt with promptly and transparently. Careful records should be kept.

## P4.1 Informal mediation

Experience has shown that many concerns can be resolved informally and locally. Such a situation might involve the person making the allegations discussing their concerns with a line manager, a member of the clergy or someone else in a position of authority, for example a churchwarden. The informal route should always be tried first. It should be clear in each parish to whom someone should go with a complaint.

At this early stage it will be important for someone to listen carefully to the complainant to determine how he or she wishes to proceed. It will also be important to try to ascertain whether a criminal offence has been committed. If an offence is suspected the complainant should be given the opportunity to make a statement to the police. If it appears that a criminal offence might have been committed the alleged offender should not be spoken to without police agreement.

## P4.2 Clergy and those holding the bishop's licence

Complaints against clergy and lay ministers holding the bishop's licence should be referred to the bishop, either directly or through the archdeacon or warden of Readers as appropriate. If the complainant wishes to make a formal complaint against a member of the clergy under the Clergy Discipline Measure 2003,[20] the procedure is fully explained in the Code of Practice to the Measure.

## P4.3 Employees

Since 1 October 2004, employers have been required[21] by law to comply with minimum dismissal and disciplinary procedures, which in most cases will involve a three-stage process:

1. The employer notifies the employee in writing of the alleged disciplinary matter and invites the employee to attend a meeting. The employee must be told the basis of the complaint and given a reasonable time to respond, and no action (except suspension) may be taken until the meeting has been held.

2. The employee must take all reasonable steps to attend the meeting, at which he or she is entitled to be accompanied. The employer must notify the employee of the decision taken and of the right to appeal.

3. If the employee notifies the employer that he or she wishes to appeal, a further meeting must be held, but any disciplinary action does not have to be postponed in the meantime. The employee must take all reasonable steps to attend the appeal meeting and is, again, entitled to be accompanied. The employer must notify the employee of the decision made.

It is essential that these procedures be followed, as failure to do so will automatically render any dismissal unfair if a claim is brought in an employment tribunal. Legal advice should be sought as appropriate.

## P4.4 Volunteers

When an allegation is made against a volunteer it may be possible to resolve the concern informally, if it is not of a serious nature. For complaints of more substance, it would be good practice to follow a process similar to the statutory procedure for employees set out above. However, if a complaint is referred to the local authority or the police, consideration should be given to whether the volunteer is suspended from duty until the outcome of those investigations is known. If the investigations are inconclusive or if concerns remain, the incumbent, PCC or other body responsible for appointing the volunteer will need to consider carefully whether the suspension should be lifted, and, if so, on what conditions. Professional advice (e.g. from the diocesan registrar or diocesan risk assessment panel) should be sought as appropriate.

*Appendix 1*

# Confidentiality and information sharing

## A1.1 General duty of confidentiality

Both law and sound morals impose a general duty not to pass on information which has been received in the clear expectation that it will be treated as confidential. That duty is not absolute, however, and the courts will not intervene to restrain disclosure where (a) the information relates to a crime or other serious misconduct and (b) disclosure is in the public interest. **Thus, where a vulnerable person is judged to be at risk of significant harm or an adult is likely to harm themselves or others, usually it will be legally possible, appropriate and highly desirable to disclose relevant information to the public authorities for the sake of protecting that vulnerable person.**

If such information has been received in confidence, the person giving the information should in the first instance be encouraged to disclose it to the authorities him or herself. Alternatively, the person receiving the disclosure should ask permission to pass the information on. If this request is denied it might still be possible to pass the information to a statutory body. Government guidance relating to child protection issued in 2003 gives helpful advice, which is also relevant in the context of the protection of vulnerable adults. The guidance states:

### Disclosure in the absence of consent[22]

> The law recognises that disclosure of confidential information without consent or a court order may be justified in the public interest to prevent harm to others.
>
> The key factor in deciding whether to disclose confidential information is proportionality: is the proposed disclosure a proportionate response to the need to protect the welfare of the child? The amount of confidential information disclosed, and the number of people to whom it is disclosed, should be no more than is strictly necessary to meet the public interest in protecting the health and well-being of a child. The more sensitive the information is, the greater the child-focused need must be to justify disclosure and the greater the need to ensure that only those professionals who have to be informed receive the material.

## A1.2 Confession

It is possible that relevant information may be disclosed in the particular context of sacramental confession. Canon law constrains a priest from disclosing details of any crime or offence which is revealed in the course of formal confession;

however, there is some doubt as to whether this absolute privilege is consistent with the civil law.[23] Where a penitent's own behaviour is at issue, the priest should not only urge the person to report it to the police or local authority, but may judge it necessary to withhold absolution until this evidence of repentance has been demonstrated.

It is in everyone's interest to recognize the distinction between what is heard in formal confession (however this might take place), which is made for the quieting of conscience and intended to lead to absolution, and disclosures made in pastoral situations. For this reason, it is helpful if confessions are normally heard at advertised times or by other arrangement or in some way differentiated from a general pastoral conversation or a meeting for spiritual direction.

## A1.3 Relevant legislation

Legislation designed to safeguard the private lives of individuals has been framed to take account of the overriding need to protect the wider community against crime and serious misconduct. Nevertheless, it is important to be aware of the legal obligations which apply to those who hold sensitive information about others.

## A1.4 Data protection

Information which relates to an individual's physical or mental health, sexual life or to the commission or alleged commission of an offence is treated as sensitive personal data for the purposes of the Data Protection Act 1998. The Act restricts the use of such information, including its disclosure to third parties, without the explicit consent of the individual concerned. This presents particular difficulties where a vulnerable person is unable to give such consent by reason of mental or physical impairment. However, there is a useful provision which permits the processing of sensitive personal data where the individual cannot give consent, providing that the processing is necessary for the provision of confidential counselling, advice, support or any other service.[24] There is also an exemption that permits disclosure of personal information to the police where that disclosure is made for the purposes of preventing or detecting crime.[25]

## A1.5 Human rights

The Human Rights Act 1998 incorporated into UK law the European Convention on Human Rights, so that it is now unlawful for a public authority to act in contravention of a Convention right.

What constitutes a 'public authority' for the purposes of the 1998 Act is a developing area of the law. The most recent judicial opinion[26] suggests that (except in cases such as the conduct of a marriage where the minister can be said to be exercising a governmental function in a broad sense) a person carrying out duties within the Church of England which are simply part of the mission of the Church (such as pastoral care) is not acting as a public authority. However, this is an area on which advice should be sought from the diocesan registrar in any particular case.

Article 8 of the Convention provides that everyone has the right to respect for his private and family life, his home and his correspondence, and that a public authority may only interfere with this right where such interference is lawful and necessary for certain purposes. The most relevant of those in the context of the protection of adults are the prevention of disorder or crime, the protection of health or morals and the protection of the rights and freedoms of others. In any circumstances where Article 8 applies to a public body, there is a judgement to be made as to whether, on balance, an interference with that right by a public authority can be justified. Where allegations of abuse are concerned, the potential harm that might result from not reporting such allegations will be a relevant factor.

## A1.6 Freedom of information

No church body is a public authority for the purpose of the Freedom of Information Act 2000, and so the Act does not have any direct impact upon the church's activities. However, those sharing information with public authorities (such as local government departments and agencies) should be aware that those bodies are subject to the Act. However, information held by a public authority in connection with investigations and legal proceedings is generally exempt from public disclosure under the Act.

*Appendix 2*

# What is mistreatment, abuse or harm?

**Mistreatment** is defined in *No Secrets* as 'a violation of an individual's human and civil rights by any other person or persons'. It is any misuse of a pastoral or managerial relationship, from the most serious to less severe behaviour, which lies at its root. Mistreatment covers **abuse, bullying** and **harassment**. These categories are not watertight and can merge into one another. **Harm** is what results from mistreatment or abuse.

Abuse may be perpetrated by an individual or a group. It may be accepted or exacerbated by the culture of an institution, in which case it is described as institutional abuse. Abuse concerns the misuse of power where control and/or authority can manifest as a criminal offence.

Harassment, bullying and exploitation, discrimination and oppression are other types of behaviour which are not acceptable within church ministry.

Abuse can take place in the person's home, day centre, family home, community setting and in public places (including churches and ancillary buildings).

Domestic abuse is widespread in our society and the Church needs to respond supportively to those experiencing such abuse. See the Church of England's report *Responding to domestic abuse* (2006).

A carer might be being physically or emotionally harmed by the person they are looking after.

All those who work in regular, face-to-face contact or have responsibilities for adults or are in positions of trust should be aware of the potential for the misuse and abuse of power. Training in good practice and awareness of adult abuse and the proper recruitment of those who work in any recognized ministry on behalf of the Church is therefore essential.

The possibility of vulnerable people being harmed is not confined to their lives outside of the Church. Church workers need to be vigilant to protect vulnerable people from harm whilst they are attending worship or other meetings or activities or being visited by someone from the congregation. There is a specific range of issues that need to be addressed about church buildings, to ensure they are safe and accessible. In addition the Church has a responsibility and duty of care to ensure that all those who are closely involved with vulnerable people are behaving in safe and appropriate ways. Of course many people will be good friends of people who have impairments – it is not appropriate to try to 'legislate' their friendship, only their responsibilities when acting on behalf of the Church. All church workers have a responsibility to treat all those they minister to with respect.

## A2.1 Why does mistreatment or abuse happen?[27]

Abuse occurs for many reasons and the causes are not fully understood. The following risk factors have been identified as being associated with physical and psychological abuse (one or more may be present in any abusive situation):

- Social isolation – as those who are abused usually have fewer social contacts than those who are not abused.
- There is a history of a poor-quality long-term relationship between the abused and the abuser.
- A pattern of family violence exists. The person who abuses may have been abused when younger.
- The person who abuses is dependent upon the person they abuse for accommodation, financial or emotional support.
- The person who abuses has a history of mental health problems or a personality disorder or a substance addiction.
- In care settings abuse may be a symptom of a poorly run establishment. It appears that it is most likely to occur when staff are inadequately trained, poorly supervised, have little support from management or work in isolation.

## A2.2 Different forms of abuse

### Spiritual aspects of abuse

Churches need to be sensitive so that they do not, in their pastoral care, attempt to 'force' religious values or ideas onto people, particularly those who may be vulnerable to such practices. Within faith communities harm can be caused by the inappropriate use of religious belief or practice; this can include the misuse of the authority of leadership or penitential discipline, oppressive teaching, or intrusive healing and deliverance ministries, which may result in vulnerable people experiencing physical, emotional or sexual harm. If such inappropriate behaviour becomes harmful it should be referred for investigation in the usual way. Careful supervision and mentoring of those entrusted with the pastoral care of adults should help to prevent harm occurring in this way. Other forms of spiritual abuse include the denial to vulnerable people of the right to faith or the opportunity to grow in the knowledge and love of God.

### Physical abuse

The ill-treatment of an adult, which may or may not cause physical injury, is regarded as physical abuse. Instances might include hitting, slapping, pushing, kicking, inappropriate restraint, withholding or misuse of medication, squeezing, biting, suffocating, poisoning, drowning or killing. It could include racially or religiously motivated attacks.

A requirement for someone to work in an unsafe environment can be construed as physical abuse.

### *Possible indicators of physical abuse:*[28]

- cuts, lacerations, puncture wounds, open wounds, bruising, welts, discolouration, black eyes, burns, broken bones and skull fractures;
- untreated injuries in various stages of healing or not properly treated;
- poor skin condition or poor skin hygiene;
- dehydration and/or malnourishment without an illness-related cause, loss of weight, soiled clothing or bedding;
- broken eyeglasses or frames, physical signs of being subjected to punishment, or signs of being restrained;
- inappropriate use of medication, overdosing or under dosing;
- the adult telling you they have been hit, slapped or mistreated.

## Emotional or psychological abuse

The use of threats or fear or the power of the carer's or other adult's position to negate the vulnerable person's independent wishes. Such behaviour can create very real emotional or psychological stress. Bullying, sexual and racial harassment would also come into this category if physical harm were not used. It includes lack of privacy or choice, denial of dignity, deprivation of social contact or deliberate isolation, making someone feel worthless, lack of love or affection, threats, verbal abuse, humiliation, blaming, controlling, pressurizing, coercion, fear, ignoring the person.

Other behaviours which may take place within a working relationship include public or unreasonable criticism, insults and shouting, ignoring a person's wishes or point of view, setting unreasonable work targets, removing areas of responsibility, undervaluing a person's efforts.

Harassment may include name calling, victimization and ostracism, unwanted sexual attention, stalking, compromising invitations or gifts, the display of images that are racially or sexually offensive, the suggestion that sexual favours might further promotion prospects.

### *Possible indicators of emotional/psychological abuse:*

- feelings of helplessness;
- hesitation in talking openly;
- implausible stories;
- confusion or disorientation;
- anger without an apparent cause;
- sudden changes in behaviour;
- the person becoming emotionally upset or agitated;
- unusual behaviour (sucking, biting or rocking);

- unexplained fear;
- denial of a situation;
- the person becoming extremely withdrawn and non-communicative or non-responsive;
- the adult telling you they are being verbally or emotionally abused.

## Financial or legal abuse

The wilful extortion or manipulation of the vulnerable person's legal or civil rights must be construed as abuse. Such activity may include misappropriation of monies or goods, the misuse of finances, property or possessions, or withholding money, the exploitation of a person's resources or embezzlement. Such abuse may involve the use of a position of authority or friendship to persuade a person to make gifts, to leave legacies or change a will.

### *Possible indicators of financial abuse:*

- signatures on cheques etc. that do not resemble the adult's signature or which are signed when the adult cannot write;
- any sudden changes in bank accounts including unexplained withdrawals of large sums of money;
- the inclusion of additional names on an adult's bank account;
- abrupt changes to or creation of wills;
- the sudden appearance of previously uninvolved relatives claiming their rights to a vulnerable person's affairs or possessions;
- the unexplained sudden transfer of assets to a family member or someone outside the family;
- numerous unpaid bills, overdue rent, when someone is supposed to be paying the bills for the vulnerable person;
- unusual concern from someone that an excessive amount of money is being expended on the care of the vulnerable person;
- lack of amenities, such as TV, personal grooming items, appropriate clothing, that the vulnerable person should be able to afford;
- the unexplained disappearance of funds or valuable possessions such as art, silverware or jewellery;
- deliberate isolation of a vulnerable person from friends and family resulting in the caregiver alone having total control.

## Neglect

Neglectful behaviour is any pattern of activity by another person, which seriously impairs an individual. Neglect can include: failure to intervene in situations where there is danger to a vulnerable person or to others, particularly when a person lacks the mental capacity to assess risk, not giving personal care, deliberately withholding visual or hearing aids, withholding food, drink, light and clothing, restricting access to medical services, denying social, religious or cultural contacts, denying contact with family, lack of appropriate supervision.

### *Possible indicators of neglect:*

- dirt, faecal or urine smell, or other health and safety hazards in the vulnerable person's living environment;
- rashes, sores, lice on the vulnerable person;
- inadequate clothing;
- untreated medical condition;
- poor personal hygiene;
- over or under medication;
- lack of assistance with eating or drinking;
- unsanitary and unclean conditions.

## Sexual abuse

A sexual act carried out without the informed consent of the other individual is abuse. Such behaviour includes contact and non-contact abuse. The issue of informed consent is a fraught one and would need to be carefully investigated. No one should enter into a sexual relationship with someone for whom they have pastoral responsibility or have a position of trust.

Non-contact abuse may include sexual remarks and suggestions, introduction to indecent material, indecent exposure.

Contact abuse may include rape, indecent assault, being forced to touch another person, sexual intercourse or being pressurized into consenting to sexual acts.

### *Possible indicators of sexual abuse:*

- bruises around the breasts or genital areas;
- unexplained venereal disease or genital infections;
- unexplained vaginal or anal bleeding;
- torn, stained or bloody underclothing;
- the vulnerable person telling you they have been sexually assaulted or raped.

### Other indications that abuse may be occurring:

- the vulnerable person may not be allowed to speak for themselves, or see others, without the caregiver (suspected abuser) being present;
- attitudes of indifference or anger towards the vulnerable person;

- family member or caregiver blames the vulnerable person (e.g. accusation that incontinence is a deliberate act);
- aggressive behaviour (threats, insults, harassment) by the caregiver towards the vulnerable person;
- previous history of abuse of others on the part of the caregiver;
- inappropriate display of affection by the caregiver;
- flirtations, coyness, etc., which might be possible indicators of an inappropriate sexual relationship;
- social isolation of the family or restriction of activity of the vulnerable person by the caregiver;
- conflicting accounts of incidents by the family, supporters or the vulnerable person;
- inappropriate or unwarranted defensiveness by the caregiver;
- indications of unusual confinement (closed off in a room, tied to furniture, change in routine or activity);
- obvious absence of assistance or attendance.

*Appendix 3*

# Examples of good and bad practice – for discussion

Most people will have no difficulty accepting the core values of independence, choice, inclusivity, privacy and respect necessary for good practice. However it is sometimes difficult to think how they might be put into practice. The following table gives some examples of good and bad practice to start discussion.[29]

| Positive Practice | Bad Practice |
|---|---|
| Being careful of our language. Always use positive language, for example, a person has a physical, mental or learning disability. | Maintaining a 'them' and 'us' divide in our attitudes, speech and actions. By not speaking to vulnerable adults as one would other adults or by only talking about 'them' without using individuals' names. Avoid using 'handicapped' or 'retarded', for example. |
| Treat vulnerable adults with the same respect as you would when speaking to or about anyone else. Always refer to them by name, e.g. 'We must remember to save a seat so Bill can join in.' | By not speaking to or about vulnerable adults as one would other adults. Grouping people together as if they are all the same removes their individuality. |
| Use proper sign language for the deaf and for those with learning difficulties. | Using action songs as a substitute for signing is wrong. The 'actions' are not necessarily intelligible to deaf people or those with learning difficulties. They may be fun but actions don't use the words; they are also fine for children or as an aid to worship. |
| Make sure everyone can get to where the coffee is served and that they receive the necessary books or papers on arrival at church. Clear access to enable independence is always the preferred option, but remember to be available to offer help should it be needed. | Assuming that the person with a disability has no need of books, etc. Assuming that all disabled people have to be served and cannot help themselves or express a choice or preference. |

| | |
|---|---|
| Giving the same respect as to others. Always knocking on the door before entering a room or home. Asking permission to join them; respecting their home and possessions. | Touching or moving personal possessions without permission. Many people rely on familiarity as navigational aids around their homes. Tidying up without permission. |
| Respecting differences – be it in appearance, ability or ideas. | Attempting to change someone's appearance to a more acceptable style. Assuming that odd or challenging behaviour is a sign of demon possession. Piling on the guilt by expressing views about sickness, disability or behaviour being marks of sin or demon possession. Imposing 'ministry' on vulnerable adults without their informed permission. Assuming that everyone shares your Christian values. |
| Make sure that everyone has access to all the projected words, pictures and presentations by offering seating with a clear 'sight line' by, for example, offering seats near the front (if they are wanted). Have more than one screen for OHPs or PowerPoint presentations and ensure that the images are not adversely affected by light, or provide written copies. | Ignoring or excluding people from everyday events or special occasions either by not inviting them or by not making communication possible. Ignoring people that are below your eye-level by only talking to their companions who may be on your eye-level. Standing whilst talking to someone in a wheelchair assumes you are talking down to them (even if you aren't) and makes two-way communication difficult. |
| Have a proper conversation using appropriate language. Ask about interests and hobbies. | Using euphemisms, irony and some jokes with some vulnerable adults can sometimes be misunderstood and your true meaning will not be grasped or it may be felt to be offensive. Just because someone has a disability it doesn't mean they can't hold an adult conversation with you – it's important not to talk in childish language. |
| Vulnerable adults sometimes welcome physical contact, but remember to ask first. Not withholding physical contact because someone has a disability. | Hugging people without asking can cause distress; people who have disabilities have preferences too. Leaving a disabled person out of 'hugging' or handshakes can be very rejecting and hurtful. |

| | |
|---|---|
| Check the building for accessibility. This doesn't only mean doors, steps and toilets, but also includes sight lines, lighting, acoustics, etc. | Failing to see that we all have similar needs. |
| Respect for dignity and feelings. Ask about personal preferences, forms of address and how much help might be needed. | Excluding vulnerable adults from events like funerals because, in your opinion, it may be upsetting. Assuming that help is needed all the time with everything. |
| Remember the needs of carers for breaks and short times apart (they may want to go to the shops or the person cared for may welcome the chance to go shopping without their carer – it gives something different to talk about on return home). | Being insensitive or neglectful of the emotional needs of carers. Judging how they spend their time or money. |

# Resources

## Resources for people who may be vulnerable

### Useful organizations

**Action on Elder Abuse**
Tel. 080 8808 8141
http://www.elderabuse.org.uk
Support, helpline and training materials.

**Age Concern England**
Astral House
1268 London Road
London
SW16 4ER
http://www.ageconcern.org.uk
A national organization offering advice and information about issues concerning older people. There are also local groups offering support and advocacy services.

**Alzheimer's Society**
Alzheimer's Society
Gordon House
10 Greencoat Place
London SW1P 1PH
http://www.alzheimers.org.uk
A national organization, concerned with people who have dementia, with local groups and a web site providing support to families and training.

**Church Action on Disability** (CHAD)
CHAD
PO Box 10918
Birmingham
B14 7YD
Tel. 0807 243 0678
http://www.chaduk.org

**Help the Aged**
207–221 Pentonville Road
London
N1 9VZ
Tel. 020 7278 1114
http://www.helptheaged.org.uk
A national organization offering advice and advocacy.

**MENCAP** (Royal Mencap Society)
123 Golden Lane
London
EC1Y 0RT
http://www.mencap.org.uk
A national organization providing services for people with learning disabilities. They also provide local groups and a web site offering support and social activities to families, adults and children.

**MIND** (The national association for Mental Health)
15–19 Broadway
London
E15 4BQ
Tel. 020 8519 2122
http://www.mind.org.uk
A national organization, web site and local groups offering support to families and sometimes direct services.

**Royal National Institute for the Blind** (RNIB)
105 Judd Street
London
WC1H 9NE
http://www.rnib.org.uk
A national organization focusing on the needs of blind and partially sighted people. They offer advice, aids and equipment.

**Royal National Institute for Deaf People** (RNID)
19–23 Featherstone Street
London
EC1Y 8SL
http://www.rnid.org.uk
A national organization raising awareness of deafness, hearing loss and tinnitus. They also train and provide interpreters.

**Scope**
PO Box 833
Milton Keynes
MK12 5NY
htpp://www.scope.org.uk
The main national organization for those with cerebral palsy, offering advice and information which can also be helpful for those with other physical disabilities.

**The Shaftesbury Society**
Shaftesbury Society
16 Kinston Road
London SW19 1JZ
http://www.shaftesburysociety.org.uk
An interdenominational body working with disabled people to help achieve social inclusion, empowerment and justice.

**Through the Roof**
PO Box 353
Epsom
Surrey
KT18 5WS
http://www.throughtheroof.org
A Christian body which aims to equip and train churches to become more inclusive of disabled people by encouraging and equipping disabled people for leadership in the church, providing support and fellowship to disabled people. This is also the contact point for the **Churches for All** consortium – a campaign to encourage churches to provide greater access for disabled people.

## A selection of useful books and web sites

Baptist Union of Great Britain, *Safe to Belong*, 2006. A policy on vulnerable adults, workbook and training materials. Available from BUGB, 129 Broadway, Didcot, Oxfordshire OX11 8RT.

The **BBC web site** has a special section on disability issues http://www.bbc.co.uk/ouch/

Hammond, Gaynor, and Treetops, Jackie, *The Wells of Life: moments of worship with people with dementia* (pub. 2004). Obtainable from Faith in Elderly People Leeds, c/o Gaynor Hammond, 29 Silverdale Avenue, Guiseley, Leeds LS20 8BD.

Jewel, Albert (ed.), *Older People and the Church*, Methodist Publishing House, 2001.

Litchfield, Kate, *Tend my Flock*, Canterbury Press, forthcoming (2006).

*No Secrets*, Department of Health, 2000. Available from Department of Health, PO Box 777, London SE1 6XH or from http://www.dh.gov.uk/scg/nosecrets.htm.

*Promoting Mental Health.* A resource for spiritual and pastoral care (published by the Church of England Archbishops' Council), this has useful material for guidance on worshipping with and receiving people with mental health problems in the Church. It has an extensive resources section:
http://www.mentality.org.uk/ParishResource.pdf

Restall, Mark, *Volunteers and the Law*, Volunteering England, 2005.

Volunteering England also have a helpful web site:
http://www.volunteeringengland.org

*Safeguarding Adults: a national framework of standards for good practice and outcomes in adult protection work*, ADSS, 2005.

### Training materials

Training materials can be obtained from your local authority, Action for Elder Abuse and the Baptist Church of Great Britain amongst others.

## Resources for adult survivors of abuse

### Useful organizations

**Women's Aid**
24-hour National Helpline: Tel.
08457 023468
http://www.womensaid.org.uk

**Respond**
3rd Floor
24–32 Stephenson Way
London
NW1 2HD
Tel. 0808 808 0700
http://www.respond.org.uk
Support for those with learning difficulties who have been abused.

**Survivors UK**
2 Leathermarket Street
London
SE1 3HN
http://www.survivors.org.uk
Support for male survivors.

**NAPAC**
Tel. 0800 085 3330
http://www.napac.org.uk
Telephone helpline for adults abused as children.

**Minister and clergy sexual abuse survivors (MACSAS)**
PO Box 46933
London
E8 1XA
Support for people sexually abused by those in ministry.

**Christian Survivors of Sexual Abuse (CSSA)**
C/o 38 Sydenham Villa Road
Cheltenham
Glos.
GL52 6DZ
Support, self-help groups, retreats, worship.

**S:Vox**
C/o St James Church
236 Mitcham Lane,
London
SW16 6NT
http://www.svox.org.uk
Support and self-help for survivors of all kinds of abuse.

## A selection of recent books and web sites

Ainsclough, Carolyn, and Toon, Kay, *Breaking Free* workbook, Sheldon Press, 2000.

Atkinson, Sue, *Breaking the Chains of Abuse*, Lion Hudson, 2006.

Chevous, Jane, *From Silence to Sanctuary*, SPCK, 2004. (Includes a comprehensive resources section.)

Kelly, Robert A., and Maxted, Fay, *The Survivor's Guide*, Rugby RoSA, 2005. Includes a resources section. Available from the Survivors Trust.

*Time for Action: sexual abuse, the Churches and a new dawn for survivors*, 2002. Churches Together in Britain and Ireland, 31 Great Smith Street, London SW1P 3BN.

**http://www.dabsbooks.co.uk**
A book service offering resources related to childhood abuse.

For information, contacts and advice about spiritual abuse, as well as other forms of bullying, it is worth looking at **http://www.bullyonline.org**
This site has links to other sites that are specific to spiritual abuse, counselling resources, etc.

# Notes

1 The Care Standards Act 2000 provides minimum standards for the residential, domiciliary or other services for vulnerable people. It includes vetting arrangements for those working with certain vulnerable people. *No Secrets* (Department of Health, 2000) is the accompanying government guidance. *Safeguarding Adults: a national framework of standards for good practice and outcomes in adult protection work* (ADSS, 2005) updates and expands *No Secrets*.

2 See The Children Act 1989.

3 See Section P2.1 for information on significant harm.

4 See Section P1.3 for the CRB definition.

5 See *Safeguarding Adults* (2005), p. 5.

6 See Appendix 2.2 for examples of mistreatment and abuse.

7 With thanks to the Rt Revd Dr David Atkinson, Bishop of Thetford.

8 The Human Rights Act 1998 includes Article 2 'The right to life', Article 3 'Freedom from torture' (including humiliating and degrading treatment) and Article 8 'The right to family life' (one that sustains the individual).

9 Local authorities have for the most part separated children's and adult services. Titles may vary from place to place.

10 See Section P2.1 What degree of abuse justifies referral to the local authority?

11 See the Church of England report *Time to Heal* (2000) for guidelines of good practice.

12 With thanks to members of the Church of England Survivors Consultation Group for this contribution.

13 See http://www.rapecrisis.co.uk.

14 D. Finkelhor, 'The international epidemiology of child sexual abuse', *Child Abuse and Neglect* 18, 1994, pp. 409–417.

15 A. W. Baker and S. P. Duncan, 'Child sexual abuse: A study of prevalence in Great Britain', *Child Abuse and Neglect* 9, 1985, pp. 457–67.

16 M. A. Chrnalogar, *Twisted Scriptures: breaking free from churches that abuse*, Zondervan, 2000.

17 This may soon be called the adults barred list. It is a register of those barred by the Department of Health from working with vulnerable adults.

18 *No Secrets* (2000), section 2.18, p. 12.

19 Some of this material was originally provided by The Churches Child Protection Advisory Service and the Lucy Faithfull Foundation.

20 The procedure is fully explained on the Clergy Discipline web site: http://www.cofe.anglican.org/about/churchlawlegis/clergydiscipline

21 Employment Act 2002 (Dispute Resolution) Regulations 2004.

22 *What to do if you're worried a child is being abused*, Department of Health, 2003, Appendix 3, sections 10 and 11.

23 This, and other issues relating to confidentiality, are given detailed consideration by the Legal Advisory Commission in its opinion entitled 'The Clergy and Confidentiality' (May 2002), to be published in the forthcoming edition of *Legal Opinions concerning the Church of England.*

24 Data Protection (Processing Sensitive Personal Data) Order 2000. Schedule para. 4.

25 Data Protection Act 1998 s29(1).

26 The judgement of the House of Lords in *Parochial Church Council of Aston Cantlow and Wilmcote with Billesley, Warwickshire v Wallbank and another* delivered on 26 June 2003.

27 Taken with thanks from the Church of England report, *Responding to Domestic Abuse*, Church House Publishing, 2006.

28 Amended from work on elder abuse by James Woodward.

29 Taken from material in *Safe to Belong*, with grateful thanks to the Baptist Union of Great Britain.